Your Turn

Write as many words as you can
that have to do with the word below.

Name _____

you

Write as many words as you can
that have to do with the word below.

Name _____

hobbies

I Can Spell and Rhyme

Brighter Child®
An imprint of Carson-Dellosa Publishing LLC
P.O. Box 35665
Greensboro, NC 27425 USA

Printed in the USA • All rights reserved.   ISBN 978-0-7696-4898-3

02-259111151

Practice by tracing the lines.

Name ALYSSA

3

Practice by tracing the lines.

Name ALYSSA

4

Practice by tracing the lines.

Name ALYSSA

Practice by tracing the lines.

Name _____

Practice by tracing the lines.

Name _____

Let's Warm Up!

Practice by tracing the lines.

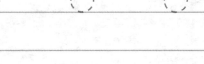

Name _____

Alphabet Review

Trace and write the UPPERCASE alphabet.

Name _____

A B C D E F G H I

J K L M N O P Q

R S T U V W X Y Z

Trace and write the lowercase alphabet.

Name _____

a b c d e f g h i

j k l m n o p q

r s t u v w x y z

Say the words.
Trace and write the words.

Name _____

ant

apple

alligator

Beginning Sounds: Letter *b*

Say the words.
Trace and write the words.

Name _____

bat

ball

bear

Say the words.
Trace and write the words.

Name _____

cat

cup

carrot

Say the words.
Trace and write the words.

Name _____

dog

doll

duck

Beginning Sounds: Letter *e*

Say the words.
Trace and write the words.

Name _____

egg

elbow

elephant

15

Say the words.
Trace and write the words.

Name _____

fish

frog

football

Say the words.
Trace and write the words.

Name _____

goat

game

girl

Beginning Sounds: Letter *h*

Say the words.
Trace and write the words.

Name _____

hat

house

horse

Say the words.
Trace and write the words.

Name _____

ink

igloo

itch

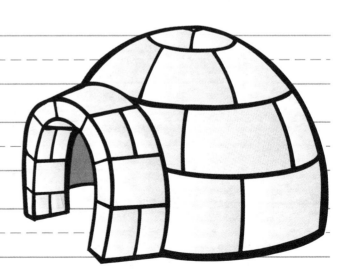

Beginning Sounds: Letter *j*

Say the words.
Trace and write the words.

jet

jar

jump

Beginning Sounds: Letter *k*

Say the words.
Trace and write the words.

Name _____

key

kite

kangaroo

Say the words.
Trace and write the words.

Name _____

lion

lamp

lock

Name _____

Say the words.
Trace and write the words.

milk

mouse

monkey

Beginning Sounds: Letter *n*

Say the words.
Trace and write the words.

Name _____

nest

nose

nine

Say the words.
Trace and write the words.

Name _____

ox

otter

octopus

Say the words.
Trace and write the words.

Name _____

pig

pen

puppy

Say the words.
Trace and write the words.

Name _____

queen

quilt

quarter

Beginning Sounds: Letter *r*

Say the words.
Trace and write the words.

Name _____

ring

rabbit

robot

Say the words.
Trace and write the words.

Name _____

sun

seal

snake

Beginning Sounds: Letter *t*

Say the words.
Trace and write the words.

top

tent

turtle

Say the words.
Trace and write the words.

Name _____

up

under

umbrella

Say the words.
Trace and write the words.

Name _____

van

vase

vest

Say the words.
Trace and write the words.

Name _____

wig

web

wagon

Beginning Sounds: Letter x

Say the words.
Trace and write the words.

Name _____

fox

box

mix

Beginning Sounds: Letter y

Say the words.
Trace and write the words.

Name _____

yard

yarn

yo yo

35

Say the words.
Trace and write the words.

Name _____

zoo

zipper

zebra

Say the words that have the short **a** sound.
Trace and write the words.

Name _____

cat   hat

can   man

bag   tag

Short e

Say the words that have the short **e** sound.
Trace and write the words.

Name _____

ten   hen

leg   peg

jet   net

Short *i*

Say the words that have the short **i** sound.
Trace and write the words.

Name _____

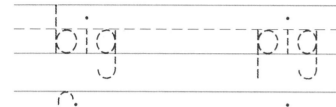

big   pig

fin   pin

bib   crib

39

Say the words that have the short **o** sound.
Trace and write the words.

Name _____

mop   hop

hot   pot

log   frog

Short *u*

Say the words that have the short **u** sound.
Trace and write the words.

Name _____

cup   pup

bun   sun

cub   tub

Say the words that have the long **a** sound.
Trace and write the words.

Name _____

bake   cake

same   game

skate   gate

Say the words that have the long **e** sound.
Trace and write the words.

Name _____

beet   feet

bee   tree

meat   seat

Long *i*

Say the words that have the long **i** sound.
Trace and write the words.

Name _____

bite   kite

mice   ice

fire   tire

Say the words that have the long **o** sound.
Trace and write the words.

Name _____

boat   goat

cone   bone

rose   nose

Say the words that have the long **u** sound.
Trace and write the words.

Name _____

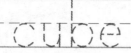

tube   cube

tune   June

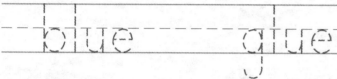

blue   glue

Say the words in the **ing** word family.
Trace and write the words.

Name _____

ring   sing

wing   bring

king   thing

Rhymes With *Car*

Say the words in the **ar** word family.
Trace and write the words.

Name _____

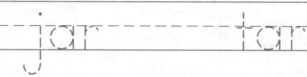

car   far

jar   tar

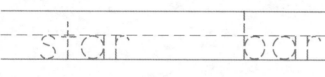

star   bar

Say the words in the **y** word family.
Trace and write the words.

Name _____

fly   cry

try   by

fry   my

Say the words in the **est** word family.
Trace and write the words.

Name _____

best   west

vest   nest

pest   rest

Rhymes With *Cake*

Say the words in the **ake** word family.
Trace and write the words.

cake   lake

bake   make

take   flake

rake   snake

wake   shake

BRRR

51

Rhymes With *Rug*

Say the words in the **ug** word family.
Trace and write the words.

rug   bug

tug   hug

mug   dug

Rhymes With *Ham*

Say the words in the **am** word family.
Trace and write the words.

Name _____

ham   ram

lamb   yam

swam   clam

jam   slam

Rhymes With *Beet* and *Beat*

Say the words in the **eet** and **eat** word families.
Trace and write the words.

Name _____

beet   feet

eat   meat

heat   meet

neat   beat

sweet   treat

Rhymes With *Ink*

Say the words in the **ink** word family.
Trace and write the words.

ink   think

link   drink

rink   sink

pink   wink

blink   stink

Say the words in the **ide** word family.
Trace and write the words.

Name _____

slide   ride

bride   tide

hide   side

wide   glide

Rhymes With *Duck*

Say the words in the **uck** word family.
Trace and write the words.

Name _____

duck   luck

truck   puck

stuck   tuck

buck   cluck

Rhymes With *Hound*

Say the words in the **ound** word family.
Trace and write the words.

Name _____

hound   bound

mound   sound

round   found

pound   ground

Rhymes With *Friend*

Say the words in the **end** word family.
Trace and write the words.

friend   end

bend   mend

send   lend

spend   blend

Rhymes With *Stop*

Say the words in the **op** word family.
Trace and write the words.

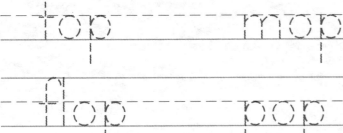

stop   hop

top   mop

flop   pop

drop   shop

Rhymes With *Horn*

Say the words in the **orn** word family.
Trace and write the words.

Name _____

horn   corn

born   torn

worn   thorn

Rhymes With *Hum* and *Come*

Say the words in the **um** and **ome** word families.
Trace and write the words.

hum   sum

gum   drum

plum   thumb

some   come

Rhymes With *Skunk*

Say the words in the **unk** word family.
Trace and write the words.

Name _____

skunk   sunk

dunk   hunk

junk   trunk

bunk   chunk

Rhymes With *Light*

Say the words in the **ight** word family.
Trace and write the words.

Name _____

light   bright

sight   night

fight   flight

might   right

Rhymes With *Mine*

Say the words in the **ine** word family.
Trace and write the words.

Name _____

mine   fine

nine   line

dine   vine

pine   shine

Rhymes With *Cap*

Say the words in the **ap** word family.
Trace and write the words.

Name _____

cap   tap

flap   map

sap   clap

tap   nap

wrap   yap

Say the words in the **ip** word family.
Trace and write the words.

Name _____

hip   sip

tip   lip

nip   rip

clip   trip

chip   dip

ship   skip

Say the words in the **ock** word family.
Trace and write the words.

Name _____

sock   clock

lock   block

rock   dock

knock   flock

Fun Rhymes

Say the rhyming words.
Trace and write the words.

Name _____

barn   yarn

cork   fork

curl   girl

bird   herd

skirt   shirt

Fun Rhymes

Say the rhyming words.
Trace and write the words.

Name _____

mouse   house

goat   boat

sheep   jeep

bear   chair

fox   box

Humpty Dumpty

Read the nursery rhyme.
Trace the words. Circle the words that rhyme.

Name _____

Humpty Dumpty sat on a wall.

Humpty Dumpty had a great fall.

All the king's horses and all the

king's men

Couldn't put Humpty

together again!

Read the nursery rhyme.
Trace the words. Circle the words that rhyme.

Name _____

Little Miss Muffet

Sat on a tuffet

Eating her curds and whey.

Along came a spider

Who sat down beside her

And frightened Miss Muffet away.

Hickory, Dickory, Dock

Read the nursery rhyme.
Trace the words. Circle the words that rhyme.

Name _____

Hickory, dickory, dock.

The mouse ran up the clock.

The clock struck one.

The mouse ran down!

Hickory, dickory, dock.

Read the nursery rhyme.
Trace the words. Circle the words that rhyme.

Name _____

Jack and Jill

Went up the hill

To fetch a pail of water.

Jack fell down

And broke his crown

And Jill came tumbling after.

Peter, Peter, Pumpkin Eater

Read the nursery rhyme.
Trace the words. Circle the words that rhyme.

Name _____

Peter, Peter, pumpkin eater,

Had a wife and couldn't keep her.

He put her in a pumpkin shell,

And there he kept her very well.

Twinkle, Twinkle, Little Star

Read the nursery rhyme.
Trace the words. Circle the words that rhyme.

Name _____

Twinkle, twinkle, little star,

How I wonder what you are!

Up above the world so high,

Like a diamond in the sky.

Twinkle, twinkle, little star,

How I wonder what you are!

Hey, Diddle, Diddle

Read the nursery rhyme.
Trace the words. Circle the words that rhyme.

Name _____

Hey, diddle, diddle,

The cat and the fiddle.

The cow jumped over the moon.

The little dog laughed

To see such sport,

And the dish ran away

with the spoon.

Read the nursery rhyme.
Trace the words. Circle the words that rhyme.

Name _____

To market, to market,

To buy a fat pig.

Home again, home again, jiggety jig.

To market, to market,

To buy a fat hog.

Home again, home again, jiggety jog.

Little Jack Horner

Read the nursery rhyme.
Trace the words. Circle the words that rhyme.

Name _____

Little Jack Horner

Sat in a corner,

Eating his Christmas pie.

He stuck in his thumb

And pulled out a plum

And said, "What a good

boy am I."

Read the nursery rhyme.
Trace the words. Circle the words that rhyme.

Name _____

Mary, Mary, quite contrary,

How does your garden grow?

With silver bells and cockleshells

And pretty maids all in a row.

Your Turn

Write as many words as you can
that rhyme with the word below.

Name _____

math

Your Turn

Write as many words as you can
that rhyme with the word below.

Name _____

Tog

82

Write as many words as you can
that rhyme with the word below.

Name _____

hat

Your Turn

Write as many words as you can that rhyme with the word below.

Name _____

sand

Write as many words as you can that rhyme with the word below.

Name _____

phone

Pronouns

Say the words.
Trace and write the words.

Name _____

I

you

he

she

we

they

me

Number Words

Say the words.
Trace and write the words.

Name _____

one

two

three

four

five

six

Say the words.
Trace and write the words.

Name _____

seven

eight

nine

ten

eleven

twelve

Say the words.
Trace and write the words.

Name _____

red

blue

yellow

green

orange

Say the words.
Trace and write the words.

Name _____

black

white

gray

pink

brown

purple

Say the words.
Trace and write the words.

Name _____

Sunday

Monday

Tuesday

Wednesday

Thursday

Friday

Saturday

DAYS

Sunday
Monday
Tuesday
Wednesday
Thursday
Friday
Saturday

Months of the Year

Say the words.
Trace and write the words.

Name _____

January

February

March

April

May

June

Say the words.
Trace and write the words.

Name _____

July

August

September

October

November

December

JULY

Sight Words

Say the words.
Trace and write the words.

Name _____

and

with

can

like

for

said

had

Farm Animals

Say the words.
Trace and write the words.

Name _____

cow

sheep

chicken

horse

pig

Say the words.
Trace and write the words.

Name _____

lion

tiger

elephant

seal

giraffe

Say the words.
Trace and write the words.

Name _____

rhinoceros

hippopotamus

flamingo

koala bear

panda bear

Pets

Say the words.
Trace and write the words.

Name _____

bird

cat

dog

fish

rabbit

Emotion Words

Say the words.
Trace and write the words.

Name _____

happy

sad

angry

scared

excited

The Five Senses

Say the words.
Trace and write the words.

Name _____

see

hear

taste

touch

smell

Favorite Fruits

Say the words.
Trace and write the words.

apple

banana

orange

grape

strawberry

Favorite Vegetables

Say the words.
Trace and write the words.

Name _____

carrot

pea

bean

lettuce

tomato

Say the words.
Trace and write the words.

Name _____

doll

truck

blocks

bear

ball

Say the words.
Trace and write the words.

Name _____

eggs

toast

cereal

milk

juice

Lunch Foods

Say the words.
Trace and write the words.

Name _____

sandwich

pickle

apple

yogurt

soup

Say the words.
Trace and write the words.

Name _____

meat

fish

chicken

vegetables

potatoes

salad

Say the words.
Trace and write the words.

Name _____

kitchen

refrigerator

oven

sink

stove

table

dishes

School Words

Say the words.
Trace and write the words.

Name _____

school

teacher

desk

pencil

eraser

classroom

Family Words

Say the words.
Trace and write the words.

Name _____

family

mother

father

sister

brother

baby

Family Words

Say the words.
Trace and write the words.

Name _____

grandmother

grandfather

aunt

uncle

cousin

niece

nephew

Clothing

Say the words.
Trace and write the words.

Name _____

shirt

pants

skirt

shorts

sweater

jacket

socks

Weather Words

Say the words.
Trace and write the words.

Name _____

sunny

rainy

cloudy

snowy

stormy

windy

Say the words.
Trace and write the words.

Name _____

baseball

basketball

football

volleyball

soccer

golf

tennis

Say the words.
Trace and write the words.

Name _____

skiing

hockey

ice skating

surfing

skateboarding

snowboarding

Winter Words

Say the words.
Trace and write the words.

Name _____

cold

snowflakes

hot chocolate

mittens

boots

blizzard

sled

Say the words.
Trace and write the words.

Name _____

flowers

bloom

warm

windy

songbirds

garden

Say the words.
Trace and write the words.

Name _____

hot

sunshine

beach

ice cream

vacation

sandals

Autumn Words

Say the words.
Trace and write the words.

Name _____

cool

leaves

colors

pumpkins

apple cider

sweaters

Say the words.
Trace and write the words.

Name _____

car

truck

bus

motorcycle

van

bicycle

train

Math Words

Say the words.
Trace and write the words.

add

plus

sum

subtract

minus

equals

solve

Compound Words

Say the words.
Trace and write the words.

doghouse

sometimes

backyard

lunchbox

sunglasses

upstairs

afternoon

Say the words.
Trace and write the words.

Name _____

run

jump

play

climb

slide

swing

ride

Art Words

Say the words.
Trace and write the words.

Name _____

paper

paint

glue

scissors

paintbrush

watercolors

markers

Your Turn

Write as many words as you can
that have to do with the word below.

Name _____

playground

124

Your Turn

Write as many words as you can
that have to do with the word below.

Name _____

music

Your Turn

Write as many words as you can
that have to do with the word below.

Name _____

holidays